Rosa Parks

Brave and Determined

by Jennifer Marino Walters

illustrated by Scott R. Brooks

Red Chair Press   Egremont, Massachusetts

Look! Books are produced and published by Red Chair Press:

Red Chair Press LLC   PO Box 333   South Egremont, MA 01258-0333

www.redchairpress.com

 FREE lesson guide at www.redchairpress.com/free-activities

Publisher's Cataloging-In-Publication Data

(Provided by Cassidy Cataloguing Services, Inc.)

Names: Marino Walters, Jennifer, author. | Brooks, Scott R., illustrator.

Title: Rosa Parks : brave and determined / by Jennifer Marino Walters ; illustrated by Scott R. Brooks.

Other titles: Look! books (Red Chair Press). Beginner biography

Description: Egremont, Massachusetts : Red Chair Press, [2024] | Includes index. | Interest age level: 006-009. | Summary: Rosa Parks was a Black American civil rights activist whose refusal to give up her seat on a public bus became the spark that started the civil rights movement in the United States. Because of Rosa's heroic acts seats on public transportation were opened to everyone.--Publisher.

Identifiers: ISBN: 9781643712499 (library hardcover) | 9781643712550 (softcover) | 9781643712611 (ebook) | LCCN: 2022943794

Subjects: LCSH: Parks, Rosa, 1913-2005--Juvenile literature. | African American women--Alabama-- Montgomery--Biography--Juvenile literature. | Civil rights workers--United States-- Biography--Juvenile literature. | Segregation in transportation--Alabama--Montgomery--History--20th century--Juvenile literature. | CYAC: Parks, Rosa, 1913-2005. | African American women--Alabama--Montgomery--Biography. | Civil rights workers--United States--Biography. | Segregation in transportation--Alabama--Montgomery--History--20th century. | LCGFT: Biographies. | BISAC: JUVENILE NONFICTION / Biography & Autobiography / Women. | JUVENILE NONFICTION / Biography & Autobiography / Social Activists. | JUVENILE NONFICTION / People & Places / United States / African American & Black.

Classification: LCC: F334.M753 M37 2024 | DDC: 323/.092--dc23

Photo credits: p. 4, 16, 18, 20, 22: Library of Congress

Printed in the United States of America

0324 1P CGF24

Table of Contents

Separate and Unequal

Rosa Parks was born on February 4, 1913 in Tuskegee, Alabama. She grew up on a farm in Pine Level, Alabama with her mother, brother, and grandparents.

Rosa's grandparents were former slaves who were now free. But they still faced a lot of **discrimination** based on their skin color.

At the time, **segregation** was in place in much of the South. Blacks and whites had to use separate restrooms, water fountains, libraries, and more. Black and white children could not go to the same schools.

After Rosa married Raymond Parks in 1932, she became actively involved in **civil rights** issues. In 1943, she joined the NAACP.

WHITE

COLORED

Good to Know

The NAACP, or the National Association for the Advancement of Colored People, works to promote civil rights and equality for all people.

The Fight to Vote

Voting was another way in which Blacks were treated unfairly in the South. Black people had to own property or pass **literacy** tests before they could register to vote. White people did not.

Rosa took the literacy test three times before she passed. In 1945, she finally became a registered voter.

Standing Her Ground

On December 1, 1955, Rosa was riding a city bus home from her job at a department store in Montgomery, Alabama. "Colored" passengers had to ride in a special section at the back of the bus. Rosa was sitting in the first row of that section.

When the bus filled up, the driver asked Rosa and other Black passengers to stand so white riders could sit. Rosa refused. The driver called the police, and Rosa was arrested.

A Brave Boycott

In protest, most Blacks in Montgomery chose to not ride the buses on December 5, 1955. The city buses were mostly empty. Blacks in the city were fed up with being treated so badly. That marked the beginning of the Montgomery Bus **Boycott**.

Good to Know

Rosa Parks was not the first Black person in Montgomery to refuse to give up her bus seat. Nine months earlier, 15-year-old Claudette Colvin was arrested for doing the same. So was 18-year-old Mary Louise Smith in October 1955.

The bus company and downtown businesses lost a lot of money. Rosa and other civil rights **activists** received threats. But they pushed on with the boycott. This peaceful protest lasted 381 days.

A Big Victory

On November 13, 1956, the U.S. Supreme Court ruled that segregation on public transportation was against the law. A month later, the Montgomery Bus Boycott officially ended.

Rosa and Raymond moved to Detroit, Michigan in 1957. There, Rosa continued fighting for equal rights for all people. She even worked with Martin Luther King, Jr.

A Historic Act

Rosa traveled all over the country to speak about civil rights and participate in marches. It was dangerous because many white people still opposed equal rights for Black people.

On August 6, 1965, Rosa
watched President Lyndon
Johnson sign the Voting Rights
Act. The act banned racial
discrimination in voting. Blacks
would no longer have to take
literacy tests in order to vote.

Big Honors

Rosa received many honors for her work. She won the Martin Luther King, Jr. Nonviolent Peace Prize in 1980. In 1996, President Bill Clinton awarded her the Presidential Medal of Freedom. And in 1999, she won the Congressional Gold Medal.

Good to Know

The Presidential Medal of Freedom is the highest honor awarded to a US citizen.

A Lasting Legacy

Rosa died at age 92 on October 24, 2005. She left behind a **legacy** as a symbol of the civil rights movement. Her bravery and determination sparked action that helped end racial segregation across the U.S.

Timeline: Big Dates in Rosa's Life

1913: Rosa is born in Tuskegee, Alabama.

1932: She marries Raymond Parks.

1933: Rosa graduates from high school at a time when few Black people in Alabama do.

1945: Rosa registers to vote.

1955: Rosa is arrested for not giving up her bus seat to a white man. The Montgomery Bus Boycott begins.

1956: The U.S. Supreme Court declares bus segregation unconstitutional. The bus boycott ends.

1965: The Voting Rights Act ends racial discrimination in voting.

1996: Rosa is awarded the Presidential Medal of Freedom by President Bill Clinton.

1999: Rosa is presented with the Congressional Gold Medal. TIME Magazine names her one of the most important people of the 20th Century.

2005: Rosa dies at home in Detroit of natural causes at age 92.

Words to Know

activists: people who use strong actions, like protests, to make changes in laws or society

boycott: the refusal to buy, use, or participate in something

civil rights: rights that every person should have regardless of race, gender, or religion

discrimination: unfairly treating a group of people differently from another group of people

legacy: how someone is remembered after they are gone

literacy: the ability to read and write

segregation: keeping people of different races, religions, etc. separate from each other

Learn More at the Library

(Check out these books to read with others)

Kittinger, Jo S. *Rosa's Bus: The Ride to Civil Rights.* Calkins Creek, 2017.

Parks, Rosa. *Rosa Parks: My Story.* Puffin Books, 1999.

Zeldis McDonough, Yona. *Who Was Rosa Parks?* Penguin Workshop, 2010.

Index

About the Author

Jennifer Marino Walters and her husband live with their twin boys and daughter in the Washington D.C. area. She is grateful to have role models of bravery and determination like Rosa Parks for her children.